The Proper Princess

J. Burchett and S. Vogler

Illustrated by Margaret Chamberlain

CAMBRIDGE UNIVERSITY PRESS

Cambridge Reading

General Editors
Richard Brown and Kate Ruttle

Consultant Editor
Jean Glasberg

PUBLISHED BY THE PRESS SYNDICATE OF THE UNIVERSITY OF CAMBRIDGE
The Pitt Building, Trumpington Street, Cambridge, United Kingdom

CAMBRIDGE UNIVERSITY PRESS
The Edinburgh Building, Cambridge CB2 2RU, UK   http://www.cup.cam.ac.uk
40 West 20th Street, New York, NY 10011–4211, USA   http://www.cup.org
10 Stamford Road, Oakleigh, Melbourne 3166, Australia
Ruiz de Alarcón 13, 28014 Madrid, Spain

Text © J. Burchett and S. Vogler 2000
Illustrations © Margaret Chamberlain 2000
Design by Angela Ashton

Adapted from *The Proper Princess Test* by J. Burchett and S. Vogler, published by Cambridge University Press, 1998 (ISBN 0 521 63946 8)

This book is in copyright. Subject to statutory exception and to the provisions of relevant collective licensing agreements, no reproduction of any part may take place without the written permission of Cambridge University Press.

First published 2000

Printed in the United Kingdom at the University Press, Cambridge

Typeface Concorde

A catalogue record for this book is available from the British Library

ISBN 0 521 66356 3 paperback

PERFORMANCE
For permission to give a public performance of
The Proper Princess Test, please write in the first instance to
Permissions Department, Cambridge University Press,
The Edinburgh Building, Shaftesbury Road, Cambridge CB2 2RU.

Contents

Introduction   4

Characters   5

The Play

Scene 1   A large, splendid room in King Eric's castle   7

Scene 2   The royal dining room   13

Scene 3   The royal dining room, the next morning   17

Scene 4   A state room, that afternoon   23

Scene 5   The royal dining room, that evening   25

Scene 6   A state room, the next morning   30

Scene 7   Wilfred's bedroom   34

Introduction

There are six reading parts in this play. One of the parts is for the **Narrator**, who introduces the story and describes some of the action.

If you are performing the play, then the **Narrator** could stand to one side of the stage, watching the action. Or you might choose to perform the play without this part, as it will work well on stage with just five characters.

Characters

Narrator

Queen Mabel

King Eric

Prince Wilfred   *their son*

Princess Elspeth   *a visitor to the king's castle*

Stiggins   *the butler*

Scene 1

A large, splendid room in King Eric's castle

It is night and the sounds of a rainstorm can be heard outside. **Queen Mabel** *is sitting on a throne.* **King Eric** *is reading the sports page of his newspaper.* **Wilfred** *is playing with a toy racing car.*

Narrator We proudly present the story of 'The Princess and the Pea'. I bet you think you know this story. A princess turns up at a royal palace, seeking shelter. She sleeps on a hundred mattresses, little knowing that a pea has been placed underneath them. She is very uncomfortable and tosses and turns all night, which proves she is a proper princess and can marry the prince. Well, that's what everyone is told. But that story is a load of old rubbish. This is what really happened . . .

It was a dark, stormy night and in the palace of King Eric, the royal family were settling down for a cosy chat.

Queen Wilfred, your father wants to have a talk with you.

Wilfred (*Making racing car noises*) Does he?

King (*Surprised*) Do I?

Queen (*Crossly*) Of course you do, Eric.

King (*Whispers to **Queen***) What about, Mabel?

Queen About getting rid of . . . I mean, getting Wilfred married, of course.

King About getting you married, of course.

Wilfred But I don't think I want to get married. Not yet anyway.

King Oh, right. Did you hear that, my sweet? Young Wilfred here says he doesn't think he wants to get married yet. (*Opens his newspaper again, with a sigh of relief*) That seems to be that then.

Queen Do I have to do everything round here? (*To **King***) If I'd left it to you, Eric, *we'd* never have got married.

King (*Sadly*) Indeed, my sweet.

Queen The point is, Wilfred, one day you will be king and you will need a queen. Just like your father did. Isn't that so, Eric?

King   (*Sadly*) Indeed, my sweet.

Queen   Goodness knows we've tried to find you a wife, Wilfred. There was Princess Petunia, for instance.

Wilfred   She didn't want to see my spider collection.

Queen   Well, she was only the daughter of a duke. What can you expect? Then there was that Princess Poppy. If *she* was royal, I'll eat my crown.

Wilfred   She wouldn't play tiddlywinks with me.

Queen   Princess Primrose was ever so eligible – and rich. I can't imagine why she refused to be tested.

Wilfred   And she didn't laugh at my jokes.

Queen   Well, it's just not good enough. We must get you married. Don't you agree, Eric?

King (*Mutters from behind his paper*) Arsenal five, Sheffield Wednesday –

Queen Fat lot of help we're going to get from him! Surely there must be someone suitable for you, Wilfred.

Wilfred I get on ever so well with my pen-pal, Minnie Mousanova. She's from Latvia. Her daddy's a fisherman.

Queen A fisherman? Forget it, my boy. You're a prince, and you're marrying a Proper Princess. And when I say 'proper', I mean one who will pass the Proper Princess Test.

Wilfred What's that?

Queen Well –

Narrator At that moment the door opened and Stiggins, the butler, entered.

Stiggins Your Majesties and Prince Wilfred, I am sorry to interrupt, but there is a young lady here seeking shelter. She *says* she is a princess.

Princess Elspeth enters, looking bedraggled.

Queen Heavens!

King Good grief!

Wilfred I say!

Elspeth Hello.

Scene 2

The royal dining room

Princess Elspeth, *now dry, is sitting eating at a long table.* ***Stiggins*** *is standing at her shoulder.*

Narrator Princess Elspeth tucked into a royal feast. Well, it was sausages actually. That was all the palace kitchen could manage at short notice.

Stiggins More wine, Your Highness?

Elspeth Yes please. I'm gasping after my frightful journey.

Queen, ***King*** *and* ***Wilfred*** *enter.*

Queen Are you feeling better now, my dear?

Elspeth Yes, thank you, Your Majesty. These sausages are wonderful. And it was most kind of you to offer to put me up for the night.

Stiggins Can I interest you in some ketchup, Your Highness?

Elspeth Just a dollop, thank you.

Queen   (*Whispers to **King***) Find out more about her.

King   What? . . . er . . . now then, what's your name, young miss?

Queen   We know that already, you silly man.

King   Of course. How did you get here, Princess Elspeth?

Queen She walked, you idiot. You can see that by the state of her shoes!

Elspeth My coach broke down. I've come miles in search of help. It was only by chance I stumbled upon this castle.

Queen (*Looking at **Wilfred***) It was a very lucky chance!

Stiggins Another sausage, Your Highness?

Elspeth Well, I've had fifteen . . . oh, go on then, just one more.

Wilfred I'll have one.

King I wonder if I know your father, my dear. I might have played darts with him.

Elspeth Daddy is King of Escallonia.

Queen (*Whispers to **King***) A very rich kingdom, so I hear.

King He's not in my royal darts league, though.

Queen Never mind that. Stiggins!

Stiggins Yes, Your Majesty?

Queen (*Taking **Stiggins** aside*) Have you prepared the bedchamber for our guest?

Stiggins Yes, Your Majesty.

Queen And have you followed my instructions exactly?

Stiggins To the letter, Your Majesty.

Narrator Queen Mabel put her arm firmly around Elspeth's shoulders and led her to the door.

Queen You must be exhausted, my dear. I will show you to your bedroom . . .

Scene 3

The royal dining room, the next morning

The family are having breakfast. **Wilfred** *is dipping toast in his egg.* **King Eric** *is buried in his newspaper.*

Narrator The next morning, the royal family were having breakfast in the royal dining room. Elspeth stumbled in, looking like death warmed up.

Stiggins (*Announces*) Princess Elspeth.

Narrator Queen Mabel looked up eagerly, but Wilfred carried on munching his toast soldiers.

Queen (*In a hiss*) Wilfred!

Wilfred (*Chants*) Good morning, Princess Elspeth.

Stiggins Can I help you to a kipper, Your Highness?

Elspeth (*Wearily*) No thank you, Stiggins.

Queen Come and sit next to Prince Wilfred, my dear. Did you sleep well?

Elspeth   (*Through gritted teeth*) Yes, thank you.

Queen   What a shame . . . I mean, I *am* glad. And how was the bed? I had a few extra mattresses put on specially.

Elspeth   A hundred, actually. I counted them all as I climbed up.

Stiggins Some tea, Princess Elspeth?

Elspeth Thank you, Stiggins.

Queen But was the bed comfortable?

Elspeth Forgive me. (*Yawns loudly*) It was a tiny bit . . . erm –

Queen Lumpy?

Elspeth Yes. Frankly, it was like trying to sleep on a tortoise!

King Oh, I say!

Wilfred How funny!

Elspeth I do apologise. That sounded most ungrateful.

Queen (*Leaping to her feet and knocking Wilfred's breakfast flying*) Not at all, my dear Elspeth! I knew we'd find you one day! A Proper Princess! What do you say to that, Wilfred?

Wilfred   Can I have some more toast soldiers for my eggs, please? (**Queen** *slaps* **Wilfred**) Ow! What was that for, Mumsie?

King   What's all the fuss about?

Stiggins   If I may explain, Your Majesty, it seems that Prince Wilfred is going to marry Princess Elspeth.

King   Good show. Now then, Stiggins, do you think Manchester United will win the Cup?

Stiggins   Well, Sire, since the transfer of –

Elspeth   Never mind football! What do you mean, I'm going to marry Prince Wilfred?

Queen Congratulations, my dear Elspeth. My husband and I have been searching for years to find a Proper Princess to marry our son. Stiggins placed the Royal Pea under those hundred mattresses on your bed, didn't you, Stiggins?

Stiggins Yes, Your Majesty. And every mattress was made of the finest goose feathers, Your Majesty.

Queen It has always been said that a true princess would be able to feel the Royal Pea. And you did!

Elspeth (*Angrily*) You mean that even though I'd fallen in a ditch, been chased by a flock of killer sheep and walked seventeen miles in high heels, you still carried out your silly test?

King We had to check you really are a Proper Princess. It's the done thing, you know.

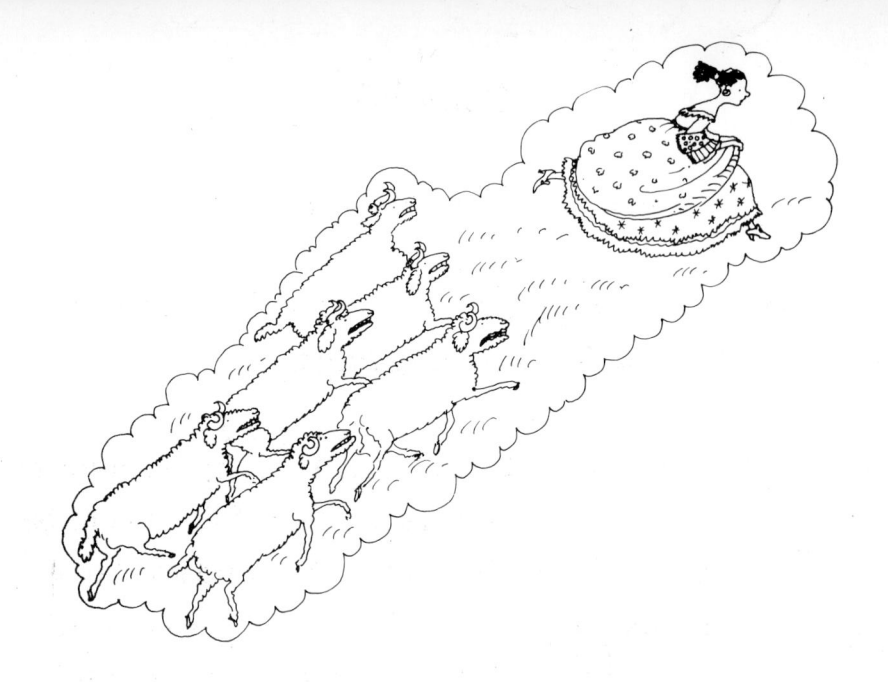

Elspeth Why didn't you look me up? I'm in the book – Elspeth, Proper Princess. I'm just after Elephant, Nellie the. And just before Ethelred the Unsteady, Royal Acrobat, By Appointment. You didn't need a test!

Queen You are overwrought, my dear. It's all the excitement of the royal wedding. Eat your cornflakes and have a doze on the sofa. (*Chuckles at her own joke*) Just one cushion this time – and no vegetables!

Elspeth Bah!

Narrator And with that, a furious Princess Elspeth flounced out of the room.

Scene 4

A state room, that afternoon

King Eric *is on the phone and* **Wilfred** *is sitting at a writing table.*

King (*On phone*) Can I speak to King Desmond? ... Des, extraordinary news! Wilfred is to be married. Yes, Mabel finally found someone to take the boy on. She's a Proper Princess ... Yes, one hundred mattresses and she still felt the pea. Can't wait to tell them down at the 'Dog and Duck' –

Wilfred (*Reads aloud as he writes*) To Miss Minnie Mousanova, Haddock Cottage, Latvia. Dear Minnie, how are you? I hope you are well. I am well –

King (*Dials new number*) Eric here . . . listen, Norman, we're having a wedding . . . No, not Mabel and I! It's Wilfred, he's marrying a Proper Princess –

Wilfred (*Still reading aloud*) I have a new pet. I call him Frankie and he is a frog. How is your cat? –

King . . . Yes, Norm, she felt the pea . . . Yes, there were one hundred mattresses . . . She's the daughter of the King of Escallonia, no less . . . No, he's not in our darts league . . . Wedding reception? . . . Down at the 'Dog and Duck', I hope . . . Yes, of course you and Queen Salmanella are invited –

Wilfred (*Still reading aloud*) Erm . . . I have some news. I am getting married. She is a Proper Princess. Mummy says I must be very happy . . .

Scene 5

The royal dining room, that evening

King, Queen, Wilfred and Elspeth
*are sitting at the table. **Stiggins** is in attendance.*

Narrator The royal family had no idea that Elspeth was not a happy princess. (*Whispers*) To be honest, they weren't all that bright.

Queen Now, the dress. I thought silk would be perfect, with a satin train and covered in pearls.

King What's that, my sweet?

Queen Elspeth's wedding dress, of course!

Stiggins More syllabub, Princess Elspeth? It's made with the finest prunes.

Elspeth Yes please, Stiggins. (*Turns to **Queen***) Now, if I might just say –

Stiggins Cream, Your Highness?

Elspeth Of course. (*Turns back to **Queen***) Now, if I could just have a word –

Queen   A small silver crown with a veil made from the finest lace.

Elspeth   That won't be necessary because –

Queen   Such modesty, my dear. Your gown will be the most beautiful dress ever seen.

Elspeth   Could I just . . .?

Stiggins   Nuts, Princess Elspeth?

Elspeth   (*Snatching a handful of nuts*) Now about the –

Queen   (*Interrupts*) I'm sure you and Wilfred want to get to know each other. Don't you, Wilfred?

Wilfred   Yes, Mummy.

Queen   Well, go on then.

Wilfred   Right . . . yes . . . erm –

Stiggins   More jelly, Prince Wilfred?

Wilfred (*Relieved*) Oh yummy! Thanks! (*Tucking in*)

King When have you booked the wedding for, my dear?

Queen Saturday. Three o'clock.

Stiggins (*Gasps*) Saturday? Three o'clock? But Your Majesty!

King (*Horrified*) My dear, that's the Cup Final!

Queen The wedding's on Saturday and that's that. The archbishop is redecorating the cathedral specially.

Elspeth This is all very kind but –

Queen I have seven bridesmaids lined up, and I've invited two thousand guests to the reception.

King I was hoping we could have it in the back room of the 'Dog and Duck'. There'll be time for a darts match between the speeches.

Stiggins   Indeed, Your Majesty. And perhaps a game of bar billiards?

Queen   (*Firmly*) The reception will be here at the palace. There will be five orchestras and –

Elspeth   Stop right there!

Queen   Pardon?

Elspeth   I am not prepared to discuss any wedding plans!

There is a shocked silence.

King   Oh, I say!

Wilfred (*Spitting out jelly*) Gosh! You interrupted Mummy!

Queen I forgive you, Elspeth. (*Stands up*) You obviously have pre-wedding nerves. Don't worry your pretty little head about the wedding plans. I'll arrange it all. Come along, everyone. Stiggins, you will phone the caterers. Wilfred, you need a haircut –

Narrator Queen Mabel swept out. King Eric and Stiggins dutifully followed. Wilfred trailed behind, still clutching his plate of dinner.

Elspeth (*Calls after them angrily*) You can't just walk out! I've got something important to say . . . They've gone! This family is completely and utterly mad. How can I get it into their thick heads that I'm not going to marry their Wilfred? I'd rather marry this walnut. (*Holds up the walnut*) . . . I say, a walnut! Now, that gives me an idea. A very good idea.

*Exit **Elspeth**, with a determined expression.*

Scene 6

A state room, the next morning

Narrator The next morning the king decided to make a few arrangements of his own for the royal wedding.

***King** and **Stiggins** approach **Elspeth**, who is sitting reading a magazine. **Elspeth** looks up.*

King Now, Elspeth, my dear, about the reception. I'm sure you'd prefer the 'Dog and Duck'. It's very cosy.

Stiggins His Majesty is quite set on the idea – he hopes to get in some darts practice at the same time.

King (*Embarrassed*) That's not the point, Stiggins.

Stiggins And he was delighted to hear that the Cup Final will be shown on the wide-screen television in the public house.

Elspeth (*Loudly*) A princess having her wedding reception in a pub! Whoever heard of such a thing?

*Enter **Queen** and **Wilfred**. **Wilfred** is reading a letter.*

King (*Hisses*) Shh! The queen might hear.

Elspeth (*Sweetly*) Good morning, Wilfred.

Wilfred (*Reads from the letter*) The weather in Latvia is very fine. My cat is very well –

Queen (*In a whisper and nudging **Wilfred***) Say something nice to Elspeth, like I told you.

Wilfred Oh, hello, Elspeth. I've had a letter from my pen-pal in Latvia.

Elspeth How nice, Wilfred. Did you sleep well?

Wilfred (*Still reading his letter*) Latvia is very pretty in the spring. (***Queen** kicks **Wilfred**'s shin*) Ow! Why did you do that, Mummy?

Queen Silly boy, it was only a nudge. Now put down your letter and answer dear Elspeth. How did you sleep?

Wilfred   Like a log, my precious.

Queen   (*Whispers to **King***) It's going to be all right. We'll have no more trouble from her.

Elspeth   And your bed, Wilfie dear, was it comfortable?

Stiggins   (*Offended*) I should hope so, Your Highness. I made it myself.

Wilfred   Never had a better night's kip!

Elspeth   (*Coldly*) I see. (*Stands up*) Right then. I'll be on my way. Thank you for having me. If any of you are near my castle, *don't* bother to look me up. (*Makes for the door*) Stiggins, the door, if you please.

Stiggins (*Worried*) Yes, Your Highness.

King What the blazes?

Queen What on earth?

Wilfred What's going on?

Elspeth Don't you know? Then let me explain. No, much better, let me show you. Follow me, everyone.

Narrator The royal family were too surprised to protest. They followed Elspeth, who led them to Prince Wilfred's bedroom.

Scene 7

Wilfred's bedroom

***King, Queen, Elspeth, Wilfred** and **Stiggins** are standing round Wilfred's bed.*

Elspeth   Seeing as no-one asked *me* about the wedding, I decided to sort it out for myself. Look!

Narrator   Elspeth lifted the corner of Wilfred's matress.

Queen   What is the meaning of this?

Stiggins   Excuse me, Your Majesty, but it appears to be a fruit and nut assortment.

King   Why have you got those under there, Wilfred?

Wilfred   I didn't put them there – but they'll be jolly handy if I get peckish in the night! Was this your idea, Stiggins?

Stiggins   (*Pulling out a notepad and pencil*) No, Your Highness, but if you would like to place a regular order – ?

Elspeth (*Crossly*) It was me! I put them there!

Wilfred Thank you, Elspeth. Very thoughtful, I'm sure.

Elspeth They weren't a snack, they were a test.
If you will only marry a real princess, then
it's only fair that I should marry a real prince.

Queen (*In a huff*) Of course Wilfred is a real prince!

Elspeth Oh no he's not. I put this lot under his mattress and he slept like a log. He didn't feel the Royal Walnut, the Royal Almonds or the Royal Pineapple! He didn't pass the Proper Prince Test. I'll see myself out, Stiggins.

Stiggins Yes, Your Highness.

King But where are you going?

Elspeth I'm going off to live happily ever after.

Exit a triumphant **Princess Elspeth**, *slamming the door behind her. The family is standing aghast.* **Queen Mabel** *is opening and closing her mouth like a goldfish.* **Stiggins** *begins to gather up the fruit and nuts.*

Narrator And Princess Elspeth left and did indeed live happily ever after. But that's not the end of the story . . .

Queen What are we going to do? I've booked the cathedral. I've ordered the flowers. I've even got your father to buy a new suit.

Wilfred (*Decisively*) Well, I don't know about you but I'm going to pack. Where's my toothbrush, Stiggins?

Stiggins (*Dropping the fruit*) I'll fetch it, Sire.

Queen Pack? What are you going on about? You really are the most stupid –

Wilfred   I'm fed up with doing what *you* say, Mother. Shut up and listen for a change. If I'm not a Proper Prince, I can marry the girl of my choice.

King   But you don't know any girls.

Wilfred   Yes I do. I'm off to Latvia to propose to Min.

Queen   (*Shouting*) To whom?

Wilfred   Minnie Mousanova, my pen-pal. Must dash. Stiggins, I'll need a map of Latvia and my arctic tent.

Stiggins   At once, Your Highness.

King   I don't even know where Latvia is!

Stiggins   It's just next to Estonia, Your Majesty.

King   (*Confused*) Ah yes, of course.

Queen But you can't marry the daughter of a fisherman. What will Queen Salmanella say, and Queen Flossinda? Not to mention Grand Duchess Grizelda. I've told them all that you're marrying a Proper Princess.

Wilfred Don't worry about that, Mother. Must dash. Toodle pip!

***Wilfred** swaggers out, head high. **Queen Mabel** collapses in a chair. **Stiggins** fans her with his notepad. **King Eric** pulls his darts out of his pocket and begins to polish them hopefully.*

Narrator And they all lived happily ever after. Even Wilfred's mother. As Minnie Mousanova just happened to be allergic to peas, Queen Mabel managed to convince the Royal Mothers' Union that Princess Min was a proper princess.